EMPLOYMENT

poems

by Gina Tron

TABLE OF CONTENTS

Deli worker

i take orders
in a green polo,
its collar reeks of french fries
i churn fresh mayo into the crusty
sun-cooked cream

If He isn't around
i warn my classmates
even those in varsity jackets
to steer clear of the condiment
they nod, bloodshot eyes get it

Fetching paper plates from the hornet-ridden trailer
admiring ants peppered in wet pizza dough
scrubbing the toilet
watching a swarm of baby blue collar bees
    come and scrub
    and get yelled at by Him
    sting
    then
    fly out
    to the bushes nearby

i only eat the poutine and philly cheese on my break
    they hatch from safe freezer bags
    and are made by a lady in a hairnet
    who is always yelling at me
like He

He who
calls my makeup weird

He who
calls me a raccoon, a freak
and yet
i can only sulk
sometimes smile
sometimes even giggle, with a shake of grimace

My boss, my master
i think He wants to tie me down
to assert His dominance
and to fuck me, maybe
and not tell anybody

i am jailbait
He jokes
staring at my tight black bell bottoms,
with butterflies hovering the bells,

As i lean over to wipe down a table,
a spillage of pepper,
with a white wet rag
before He orders me to leave

You have attitude, He says
but also
you need to stick up for yourself, He says
the same as the man my friend babysits for

Both look like ministers, kind of
with glasses and brown hair,
they merge as one dark memory
a bully in the sun

and a boyfriend in the shade
well, inch of a boyfriend

i like Her because She makes jokes with me
    one month in
grey haired and lined face,
She makes me think of a grizzled Sarah Connor
of New Mexico, maybe She lived there once
Her son was in my class and when i first saw him
he was to me what a teen just is:
    cool—like Bart Simpson mixed with the Beastie Boys

She
who butters sandwiches with sun-baked mayo
tells me,
    i don't believe what they say about you
    neither does my son
Her son ends it all with a belt,
not much later in life

Beyond the Budweiser Clydesdale figurine
beyond the Nascar bees on the corner screen
i stare at a lonely tree in the window
blowing slowly in the oven air
by the roadside, rockside
lives pass in the night
through cemetery stones
green mountains in the shade
at home
hours pass in darkness
watching palm trees swaying
from the oven in my bedroom
changing channels to find them

searching for lives i want to enter
possess in wait
driving past pine trees
where i want to be,
anywhere but here.

Video transferer
/PSA maker
at a public access channel

Discretions
  i am privy to
non and in
nobody knows

my credit is nameless
from behind thick cold tar walls
with an oven of reels and sparking lights
matchbooks ignite with the memories

i feel human
in these walls
bless the Vocational Center for raising me
for allowing me to wave
my frigid virgin hands above the toxic flames
distracting me
from the paths i'm no longer allowed
to barrel down, roadblocks abound

Receptionist radiates in blue pant suits
cat jewelry and grandma perfume
she makes me think i can talk,
i can
not just smile, sulk

i'm silk

i enter my warm cave and put on the reels
let them spark up my pupils
zooming in like lime cameras, like guns
watching the secret lives of neighbors

opening presents, snowmobiling, kissing, posing
as i rip their lives off 8mm ribbons
and burn them onto ribbons of tape
plaster a sticker, "precious memories"
long and faded

A man zooming into a woman's butt
secretly in black in white,
on a fifties beach
cat eye glasses, floppy hats, and a lens—creep
i construct lava lamps, gradients
to honor church banquets and snowmobiling events
within the vaginas of living rooms
insulated in layered curtains

Flickers and clicks
the smell of dust and film
every family is lean until the 1990s
when the corn syrup wave comes
knocks us all down

i can see it upon the last month of the decade,
as it comes to transfer to a new form

Transferring teenage hopes
onto ribbons
hoping i can work alone in the kind cave
for always
instead of the harsh sunspots
i want to live in the cool black
of a movie's ending credits.

Drugstore cashier

It's a pharmacy
meant for health
so why do i
stand in front of shelves
of cigarettes
beside
rolls of gambling tickets?

A grey haired man who always wears blue
asks for a pack of Pall Malls
every day,
this is his routine, i think
i am part of his morning,
i smile
i shed sprinkles to it
have a nice day
have a great day
thanks so much, have a wonderful day
have a good evening
don't work too hard out there, see you later

Another cashier
a teen too
parrots the customers, her family, her only friends
morphing somehow into an aging bird

Not getting any younger girl, she says
it's a real rat race out there, she says
she is kind,
they all are here
even if some seem like fast forward buttons

When i stand too long
because i am not allowed to sit, ever, for some reason,
i am to stock the shelves of stool softener and M&Ms
while "I'm Not in Love" and "Cruisin' Together" blast from above
also Robbie Dupree's "Steal Away"
all songs that make me think,
i could have a house of my own in the country, a 60-something buying
lawn ornaments and stool softener at a drugstore, making small talk with
the cashier then drinking iced tea in
the sun
all songs that also make me think
of wanting to die on the road to nowhere, driving as the sun is setting,
sobbing at Shoney's
maybe that's an okay way to go
why the hell not?

A woman with a swastika tattoo on her chest
snarling beyond her spaghetti straps
yells at me when cigarette prices swell
a lady who grumbled at the markup scolds her,
do you think this KID has any control over that?

A ringlet peer with muscular arms
a stink of gardenia
cheats on her husband
at lunch time
with a young man
her son's age
blasting nu-metal, silver balls around his neck
on the way to Best Buy
where they fuck by the exit
everyone knows

A blonde in tight pants comes in to work on dope
injects herself in the bathroom
everyone knows
then the boss knows
then she vanishes

A man tries to get photos developed
of naked children
the police are called
everyone knows

i go on three dates with a man
who pillaged my AIM profile
you're a freak like me, he says
i think maybe not, but maybe
his baggy pants ripped at the bottoms, wet
he says his dad just died in 9/11
he parrots this to a Cumberland Farms cashier
until she gives him money
reluctantly, to push him out
so she can continue to sell M&Ms and cigarettes and lottery tickets
he parrots this to his roommates in the trailer
until one calls him a liar
another wants to bite me
my presence alarms her
she brags about luring men to the McDonald's parking lot
to rob them
so she can eat and swallow
that's where these pills come from, she says

When i find out his dad is still alive,
and blow up our affair
he calls and calls and calls

and sometimes the phone rings at work and i can feel him
the lady in the photo center lies
he catches on and begins coming inside
i'm not a stalker, he says, assures, yells like a megaphone
while stalking
and calling and emailing
—he's had 3 birthdays this month—
as i keep stacking and stocking
M&Ms and thermometers and lawn ornaments
and cigarettes and stool softener.

Petsmart cashier

The manager is a lot like the hamster
nice enough looking, at first
why would He bite
why would so many quit
the plastic decorations are cheery enough,
right?
the tubes in the cage
the tubes of change
stinking of iron
stinking of staring
from Him

He who looks like a minister
the kind with kids
the kind who is known as kind
the kind you will see on the front page
in cuffs —
alongside a quote about how great He is
how distraught the whole town is
how horrified the church community is
oh the horror, the horror
the whole town is in mourning
who could have seen this coming?
(everyone)

Trying only to breathe in wagging tails,
and scarlet feathers with claws
and jade feathers with claws
trying to breathe out the stares, the comments
change and a treat
here's change for you and a biscuit for your dog
can i pet your dog?

[counter wipe down,
never look down]
have an amazing night
the fish and the lizards
unaware
the others semi
—aware

One morning i show up
to open the panes
and a cage stands before me
between red and blue slides
a cherub with reflective onyx eyes
i pet him
i hold him
i take him home and name him Chunk
and within an hour
he takes a chunk out of my finger
blood rushing,
this is his true form

i pass by his cage and he pounces up
gripping the bars with his paws
gnawing, pinching
when i try to feed him
he snaps
my cat fears him

Chunk doesn't appreciate his circumstances
so he's feisty
but it changes nothing.

Stockbroker

It's either take three buses
or ride home in my coworker's Porsche
maybe my bulldog-in-stripes boss's Lamborghini
or my supervisor's red Audi
or her husband's black Audi
i will have one too, soon enough
i'm told
if you work hard, you'll have it all
if you work hard, it is impossible to fail
if you work hard
you can't not be rich, loaded

i'm just like the man in *Boiler Room*, i think
i work hard but my dad's still not proud of me
i am a junior stockbroker, a junior financial adviser
but He still calls me a telemarketer
He doesn't get it

i turn baby broker
because artistic i no longer want to seem
so i eclipse
later, a man tells me this is
the most artist thing to do
while i'm bursting at the seams
of my disgusting suit

12 hours a day on the phone
icy calls to Luke, warm to red hot expletive Luke, Sir

Hi, i'd like to offer you a free financial consultation

i think they'll be blown away and sign
i think they'll hand me their money

two peas in a grocery store do
only
get a load of this
i really am just a telemarketer
in a 300 dollar suit
going into overdraft
eating soup once a day
mangling my feet
with 29.99 shoes that don't quite fit

Is this what heels are supposed to do?
Is this why women complain?
i'm a professional now

The damage will last for years
to the bank account, the feet.
bottom of the pyramid

We work in a triangle
polyhedron off the road in an industrial park
surrounded by French signs and ladies with frizzy red hair
smoking cigarettes in yellow kitchens, soaking into gravy-drenched fries
i could be the fry, the lady, or the mansion that surrounds
her trailer, but probably just the trailer in the end
only lonely cars pass us by, no pedestrians

One in an Armani suit tells me
He is scared of me
because though i am quiet, he can tell i am always thinking
always processing
always stirring something
i laugh and tell Him He's right

be careful of those quiet ones, they always say
remember

When my supervisor is getting audited
She tells me, sign a piece of paper
that says i made 30K
i made 6.5
i made 1.33 dollars an hour, i did the math
i tell Her to fuck off
or pay me for my employment, She refuses
i tell Her i hope She gets what She deserves
i rise from field mouse to pest in the house

As always, as before, as ahead

He calls me a loser
He yells at me for making His wife cry
He doesn't care how many times
i cried on the bus, on the inside
all my spirit below the drain, just gas left
just 87 octane
siphoned out of a '93 Pontiac
while He and She raced home
in their new red Audi
running on
93 premium.

Part time teleprompter operator
to
full time technical director

i set 4 alarms
wake up at 3:30 am
drive in the dark, the tailgates my sun
it makes me feel alive
to be up this early
privileged to conscious while others dream
i am bathing in one

Scrolling words to a screen
for a news anchor i grew up hating
watching a man move buttons
when He speaks, when She speaks, when The Weatherman speaks
i want to fly, like them, with ease
onto plasma displays, living digitally
as a side piece to the news machine

A teacher sex scandal—
the cameraman man, pepper ponytail and gum
tells me
he had sex with his teacher when he was 14
no big deal, i'm proud of it, he says
she used to give me a ride home AND a ride, he says
then i give him a ride home, he has no car
can't afford one

Request box:
we're gonna need a school shooting graphic
we're gonna need a drowning graphic
we're gonna need a pie contest graphic
we're gonna need a robbery map

Even if you fuck up,
just remember it's just the news
it's not an operating table, He says
we report damaged bodies, we don't make them
we certainly don't save them from sickness, from death
we aren't doctors but the sense of humor, well
it's gonna be like you are
it's gotta be like you are
that will save your life

An ambulance chaser, a nightcrawler in suspenders
with sirens on his pickup, *tv news* scrawled upon its bed
delivers tapes of mangled trucks and humans
the jaws of life
biting under fog and dew
in twilight

The morning crew
in the control room
is only men,
they treat me like one too
one enjoys that i am not
but keeps that thought
shut like a window
open just a crack

i fly into it full time
night shift, also only men
minus flutters of part-time femininity
rolling decks
delicately
pushing buttons
like butterflies

as the news is created

i used to be a model, one says
echoing memories of Rodeo Drive
yarns of celebrities trying to catch her with a net
she drags me out to her car one day to listen to a song
she says is about her
my name is in this song, she says
i don't hear it

The Master of Control tells me,
someone once had a heart attack
during the evening news
while running graphics
the show must always go on, He says

His eyes are wet
whisky on His breath
His whisker hair soaked in cigarettes
puffed in the lounge,
red rugged like a carpeted shining elevator
no windows

The only window
in my world
reveals the sky of the studio
grids and fresnels and accordions
where the show must go on
a cog in the machine showing
who's who in getting arrested
this evening, this week, an endless cycle
of showing
who's who in succumbing to thorns about town

i have to stop saying i hate the media
because i am the media,
just a tiny little camera in a sea of them
but still

i fly up so fast
to the light
& can tell why
man who looks like child predator in *Happiness*
tells me i look sexy today
grandpa man tells me
i look sexy today
married man tells me
i look sexy today; tell me your perfume
so I can tell my wife

i am so good
i am so talented
says the director, He seems to accept me as His right-hand man
prepping me to be a He
a Director
if i flutter right
but there's a ceiling, despite the lack of windows
and it lowers when i won't lower myself

Then i am so bad
i am so not talented
a good show becomes bad
i have shifted in His bird's eye view
a walking mistake

Egg on your face, He says
suck it up

don't complain
it's a glamour job, He says
as if
working there means i'm covered
in fur and diamonds facing forward
i can only buy earrings at Claire's
if i put them on my credit card
i am sinking into overdraft's ocean
moths are just working-class butterflies
watching butterfly clips go extinct
my headband is deteriorating fast, like a burned CD-Rom in the sun
i start transforming into a worn wolf

She who fucks the director
to become a director
after witnessing my folly
while her husband melts in a vat of confusion
at their trailer-in-heat
becomes a mini-director
but still
is fed just 39.5 hours a week
just short of the kingdom
a taste, a tease of health insurance
a taste, a tease of the swiveling throne

The decided director flies in from New York
He has experience from not here
so He is paid more than twice of me
He is 2 times me
but i His trainer

His collar doesn't fit
He is not a sponge, He is a window pane

my glass is clean
still no one sees my wings
just my thighs
my many, many thighs

i am an octopus
pushing glowing buttons in the dark
master of control in the night
cramming dated tapes into machines
which glow up screens
across the counties
Simon & Simon
a man on PCP getting choked out
Dr. Phil screaming at
a man who thinks he's possessed
a child being criticized on stage
for Mom's mistakes

Mashing together images
for an above shoulder punch
a gun over police lights
embedded shadow
a knife over police lights
gradient baseball bat over a hillside
a robbery, a shooting, a stabbing,
a ballpark fundraiser, a courtroom fight,
a sick moose, a missing kayaker
from the audio booth, i direct helicopters to the studio
as my coworker hauls,
wraps the news desk in blue blankets
goodnight news
i stay alone by the big screens, in front of racks of beeps and wires

until checkout, just in time for last call:
drive in the fog, cross the border in cerebral haze
siren and lights, you work for the news?
okay, later gina

A woman pulls up to the station wearing tin foil
a woman sends flowers to the anchor
a woman needs to be restrained

A part-time He
who blushes easily, like a doll
who sails upon Dad's sea
wears button up shirts
like a soft stockbroker
resting on the cushion of His creators

He uses a clipboard as a paddle
upon my rear end
i say to myself, it didn't end in the fifties,
this is real and now, i didn't think
i guess i do now, fine i get it
this isn't a show

He says, don't worry i didn't enjoy it,
when i order Him to stop

He tells me later He missed out on His dream job
of becoming a cop,
an officer of the law between sailboat trips,
because of me,
admittedly,
on a lie detector test,
said he "sexually harassed" someone at a worksite

He uses air quotes

Egg on my butt
and egg on that clipboard too
i march out of there
but not before egging the house
it's hard to clean dried egg off carpet.

Real estate receptionist

During my interview
Her husband has me take a personality test
    He says people fit into four groups
    some are leaders like His wife
        others are simple like the ex-receptionist, you only
    ask them about family, He says

i don't remember what i was, but i don't think it's true
i can do part time work, i say
the news is not paying you enough, He asks
He says the Weather Man is always wrong about the knots in the lake
i shrug and say it's a fun job
i definitely do not deem it a glamour job

On my first day i meet His wife
    The Her
    She walks up to my desk and doesn't say hi
    She dumps a stack of papers on my desk
    tells me to file them
    i ask a question, Her eyes stab mine. Rookie mistake, a man
explains, you don't ask Her questions

Am i in a small-town real estate version of *Devil Wears Prada*?
    She looks kind of like her,
    not in real life
    but in Her picture plastered on logos on the wall
    She is blonde and full of white teeth

She *looks* as though She would be nice, i think

He slams a photocopy of a knots chart on my desk
    give this to Weatherboy, He says
    i throw it in the trash

He smiles whenever the clock moves a number
She only does in pictures
on billboards and trucks
for clients
maybe Her husband
in their BMW, at their country club
when Her crown's around her A-type head

i'm a peasant trying to speak to a Queen
punished for eye contact
maybe it's the personality test
    the results don't match me
    my emotions
    maybe my responses don't match my performance

i am mediocre here
cannot be anything more
it's what the test said

If i test the test, i get shoved back in the box
draw within the lines,
do not squiggle

Don't forget to call your mom, it's Mother's Day,
i tell Him
Don't forget to call Her
Don't forget to wash your luxury car
Don't forget

When i put in my two weeks
He transforms into a beet red doll
trying to make his BMW disappear
my wife is crying, He says

please stay four weeks
i agree

The last day
He tells me, make sure your dad calls me when he sells the house

Teddy Bear Factory assembly line

Dressing bears for spare money
during their mating season
so many mothers
receiving chocolate animals in sundresses
honey bear predators in pink robes
holding soaps and hearts and flowers
notes that all basically smile
I love you Mom, you're the best

In the assembly line
i feel like Lucille Ball in the chocolate factory
fucking up for laughs
my friend is Ethel
or perhaps she is Lucy and i am Ethel
i am told she's more attractive so
she gets to be the star and i the side
kick, no laugh track,
just the one that erupts from our team belly
ripping beheaded bears out of hibernation
impaling their dismembered limbs with sticks
no one finds us cute
though we are stuffed animals
dipping into this life
they are right
it's a trip, not a home
and it's easier to visit than live
in this building

Still,
it makes me feel alive in a different way
an actual punch and tick
i love getting to peek into
the Valentine's rain shower

a front row seat to intimacy
all its juicy, furry scandals

One order,
two bears
same outfit
both nurse bears,
two notes
two different names
two nurses
one dick
Violet, you're the only one for me, one says
Tammy, you're the only one for me, one says

Lucy and i giggle
and are scolded like cubs

i use my 50 percent off
for nightly hibernation hugs
since no mom or valentine
each seasonal shift
i gift myself a bear
a naked one. there are no outfits that fit me.

Director

No interview questions, just compliments
on my hair, my life, my path
He says, your resume looks like mine when i was your age

i start that day, the second i'm hired

i run a news wheel on the dot
a solo anchor
behind a fishbowl
fluff pieces about Chipotle
it's national but hidden
a burrito under a porch

The job is easy
everyone says i'm good
maybe it's because i'm from far away
that's what makes me look good, i've learned
i'm fresh meat, not meat with complications

Not yet

Not ever

Within 3 weeks

Emergency meeting, the company is sinking and everyone is crying
but i get a severance check for nothing
so i'm secretly smiling
no kids to feed
no spouse to answer to
just a barren bank account
a hungry will to succeed

There's an audience of people who care, i think
but the lights are out in the studio
i can't see who they are
i only have silhouettes to impress
until the light's flipped on
i'll work so hard
to make these shadows clap for me
if this building ever finds a way
to pay
its bills.

Graphic artist

i get lost in the woods of words
draped in red and fur
i submerge into the ends of movies
the tail end when it all goes black
morphing texts from one font to another
for the overhaul
i am but a peon in a sea of freelancers
but i do get credit
enough so that i am given a shot for a fulltime job

During my trial, i watch movies
to pick the most sensational images
the most violent and sexy looks
women in bras holding guns
mostly Tori Spelling handling a handgun
she's wearing lace and silk
standing in a doorway of a house with nice pillows
cursive live, laugh, love
or a covered porch with nice pillows
fearing her ex, fearing her boss, fearing her stalker,
an athlete teen on the swim teen
who comes across porn
while laying on nice pillows
living, laughing, and loving porn
his girlfriend can no longer reach him, nor mom
they cut the obsession from his organ with surgical precision
he wakes up pale and sweaty when it's removed
and loses his swim life
loses his touch
but keeps the pillows

Big juicy evergreen buttons that scream
violence and sex and rape

flagging it all down like a collision
of a third party

Smaller flags for the times of challenge,
9/11, school shootings, terrorism
rendering big-haired blondes to roll onscreen
to announce watch this, watch that

i'm watching myself do what i want
from the ceiling
never on the floor
i am tired, physically
from dipping into sensational life myself
trying to be a character in a movie
not the one making the credits
trying to be a character in a show
the main one too
not the one making the show
trying to ride both timelines

Now falling apart under snow
buried, as i work
when the sun is down
and sleep without stars
i blow it.

Technical director
at a television channel
owned by the Catholic Church

A druggie enters a Catholic channel
and a cokehead arises from the ashes
pink lines one day
white the next
showing up sleepless,
with images of slain sheep
the slaughter from the bible seeps into my skin
switchboard buttons morphing
darting into highways behind my eyes

He is melting as He trains me
i am from far, far away
He knows
i am caring more about the brain drip
the heart hornets, super stingy
than the machine that makes my money
heart bleeding colors like my brain
linking LSD and MDMA with pleasure and pain
dicing up the comedowns like a concert
licking my salty wounds, cramming them with Sour Patch Kids
sugar in a straw, granules swimming in my soul

i bleed out tears from my palms
when the floor swirls, when my friends fall into a whirlpool
after thine who went on the cross for stuck a machete into my back
my spine rises up with frickles like thick hair follicles
sharp and sick
like Benedict
a neon cross burns into my skull
the night i black out
and get sucked into a black hole

grabbing for bricks from others' walls
to rebuild my crumbling body
an over the shoulder of Pope Benedict
XVI melts too
into Jason Vorhees, cracked music
from below
// when my mom was sick
i would slow down .wav files
from our computer's encyclopedia
she'd tell me to stop because
it sounded like demons

Waiting to be fired
    i never am
    even as an asshole on acid
    from first day forward to every
    they really do forgive
    (i guess)
    even if they shun
    even though they hate
    rolling up late, always
iced coffee in hand, do not speak to me until i drink it
i am always hungover
that's my mother fucking cross to bare, to bear
they tell me to take off time
get my brain right
my spinal cross adjusted
but holy Father of mine
tells me there's no time
to enter the church rehabilitation
just pull yourself out of the situation
and get your ass back to work
making it abundantly clear

as he sends an abundance of lilies and roses
to the emergency detox altar
of bread to fatten up the sick
that i must work to not be a burden
        the disgrace i already am
at any cost
    thank you for watching my demon

The Deacon, The Holy News Director
never looks me in the eye
i peer into His office
photos of Him smiling so hard His teeth could shatter
His arm around Pluto and Goofy
in one, His wife too, an invisible chain around her neck

He looks as though He would be nice
looks as though..
but He always has fume lines above His head
a mad cartoon lab rat
for that price they better come with a blowjob, He says
re: those office chairs

Dress up the news chairs and desk and stands at night in doilies
undress them in the morning to expose the ichthys
their thong, their cheeks, their mouth
their bountiful overreaching arcs
from their blue blankies

The news anchor
likes men, likes a good sin
but the Deacon doesn't know
about this torn and normal man

i imagine him yelling at himself in the mirror
i hate you!
each and every pink-dusted day
before sitting at a desk
cameras pointed at his head like machine guns
with graphics of babies wailing from below
from the pits of the serpent women
who also make the news
much to the cross's protest
a prompter spinning neon green letters about abortion
about the sanctity of marriage
cast on a box of black
crushed diamonds in his mind
so he can shrink away and take up less
space and time
shroud of Turin

Emergency meeting called
and the big, big-big He,
who owns us
yet is still part of the flock, above most
is being arrested on child porn distribution charges
after those Thai trips
and everyone is crying
the whole community is in shock
i'm just high, and not surprised
it's cliche, really

Even if He did get involved, he must have just clicked a bad link before
getting sucked into that world, a marketing woman says
the IT director says he wishes that was true

she cries: I was watching some MTV awards show with my daughter last
week and the host was making masturbation jokes; it's no wonder that a
world as sick as this could even turn Monsignor into something bad

i push buttons
for credit cards
i press white powder
with credit cards and
on faces of priests and monsignors and anti-abortion activists
take their shine off
make them look more ghoulish
i press white powder on a ghoul
take my shine off

Prepping pro-life activists to speak to liberal media
now i could look in the mirror and say i hate you
but i don't look in the mirror
just use it to snort drugs
think of the before times

We watch a video about child sex abuse
it's required since the incident
since the many, many incidents
in a large classroom
with jello questions in their minds
religious devouts and television production stoners
sitting in a room of pray

Grizzly bears on screen growling over their prey
i try to get them to touch me before I touch them, one says
so they feel like they did it, he adds
I pick kids who are thought of as liars, one says
I target the ones from bad homes, one says

Hours before the Christmas party,
the studio collapses
as if God Herself got annoyed
with the station, with the situations,
crumpling light grid
Deacon running past
the orderly sheep
so He can see the light of the day
instead of the collapsing windowless black box
spiked and red-eyed
house in *Poltergeist*

i wear antlers at night
and dream of a man with a blind right eye
and a head wound
nightmare myself into a car with a man who has 666 carved onto his abs
sucked of purity of fairy tales
i sit on the throne in the control room
half blinded myself
tape over my mouth, hair fried
lying over the oven of the switchboard
day after day, it's like dragging myself from the pits of hell
to even get out of bed
to even breathe
iced coffee and more coffee and more
stimulants to balance out the night
the cracking moon
vodka and whiskey to balance out the sun, tearing light
always barracuda darting through my blood streams
the water is never clear, never safe.

Part time journalist

Bringing tape recorders into bars
into farmhouses
into courthouses
into halfway homes
into halfway happy homes

Tell me about the drugs you put into your arm
tell me about how your daughter was shot nine times
tell me about how you got shot
tell me what it's like to grieve
thank you for your time
have a nice day
tell me about your pain
have a beautiful evening
i'll soak it in and wring it out
try to iron it out in a way
so you won't want to kill me
so you won't lose your job
but no promises

i think i speak awkwardly
until i have to listen to myself everyday
twice, sometimes three or four times
then i decide i sound quite good
awkward moments
are all fine in real time
not at-the-time mind time
i advise everyone to record themself
you really sound fine
now tell me about the worst day of your life
line by line
sorry, i have no control over headlines

The headline an editor will choose
without really thinking of me
will for sure be the death of me
someday, literally
easily
they'll change it to something
offensive to trans people
and suction my name to it
please change this
they'll change it to something
offensive to a massacre victim's parents
please change this
they say no 80 percent of times
and i'm the asshole

Sometimes i get praise
maybe even an award
sometimes i'm called a cunt
sometimes the Governor takes notice

Sometimes i give advice:
Sometimes you're not allowed in the kratom shop anymore
sometimes a whole town thinks you're a cunt
sometimes a whole town thinks you're an angel
sometimes a whole town is mourning
sometimes the entire town wants to kill someone
collectively

i am fine with it all
whatever the response
all the accolade sprinkles
and balled up cunt quotes
will float away with the river

once they cross over the horizon
i have to forage and summon
new debris.

Creative director for fashion show

We need a fashionable bench for the press
we need to get Him off the stage
before He gets cut, and all the poison spills out
His liquid crown, His iridescent cream
like a kid peeing himself at the talent show
He brings the intern to a roof
the one who saved the show
such a little smokeshow, He says
to offer him coke—i gotta go
i will not be a part of this
i'll do coke with my equals
in the bar, just under the roof
peeling off my clothes
like an onion
jumping into a jacuzzi
peeling the layers of His retina off
like an onion
with a disco-ball emerald inside
blowing off the dust
so that every single one of the mirrors can reflect

A Wall Street Journal reporter
writes about it all
grabs me by the antlers
i first put on by the sinkhole
then laid in an even darker spot,
drags me down the hall to my bedroom
for an end-of-year kiss,
i kiss her for the sake of time
she rips all the paintings off my wall
with the most spiteful smooch
i know you don't love me, she tells me

It's true, i don't love any of this
i'd rather lie in the wilderness
if only i could contain this excitement in a ball
carrying it with me
to the cliff, the trees
i need its electricity to flow within me
if only

We have to get this event into the paper
we have to get likes, we have to be liked
if only
i cannot control, i can only steer, only imply, i reply

i want to lie in a tent
then i'll be forced to make toast from bread
the only loaf around
right now there's bread in my kitchen
i see only squiggles, they are thick
i need a machete to cut through them
i give up, order a 17.99 dollar sandwich
and sleep in a bowl of grits

i want to rip the last layer of clothing
from my body, from the thick brush
it doesn't reflect me anymore
i am tracing paper
playing ring and roses
around the lit-up shows
in this circus tunnel
smiling
but will slip and slither out
through the first hole i see.

Grocery cashier

Beep, beep, beep
when i'm behind the register
i can see the products, really *see* them
and their prices,
from apples to shredded wheat
not blurs of numbers
not abstract thoughts

When i shop i lose my feet
a floating ghost with no concept of money
i can't conjure what i need
to nurture this flesh box
why can't i transfer this into that
i want to be like those who calmly tally
the products into their register
it doesn't register for me

They say i have gifts
but some of my produce, it's mediocre, soft in spots
store brand even
bagged badly

There are sharp knives sticking out of my brain
that cut with ease, skillfully, like a smoke show
but other parts of my head are like the plains
by the Denver airport
kind of close to major activity
with ruby eyes sticking out of haunted horses
but nevertheless
still
dull in parts
and honestly kind of common.

Walmart warehouse worker

They tell me to take a pee test and i ask if weed counts
they say it does
i piss in a plastic cup
fill up a hollow Spongebob
i get the job anyway

Videos about forklifts and garbage compactors
a blonde model in a blue vest
ordering me to ignore union spokesmen
she says, I know that Walmart is my family
and they care about me. Why would I need a union?

i lift 30-pound boxes from shelves while standing on a ladder
i shoot at prices
i make prices
i blend into aisles
i am a bottle of stool softener

Coworker reeks of impending death
6 years younger
and 16 teeth less
16 inches thinner around the waistline
a studded belt
she sticks to me

i overhear blue vests throwing boxes to another
like tennis but meaty
Jim broke his arm last night, one says
he's gonna get disability now; he's made it, the other says
i'm scared to break my arm
break a leg

i get a story published in the Washington Post

about pee tests, weed tests
thanks Walmart for this
literary leg
this inspiration from a blue hell

Wow, you've really made it, they say
i'm living on two timelines
which one is the lie?
which one is the truth?
both and both i think,
only one person knows i work at Walmart
they see me drunk
in the hot tub drowning in bubbles
to heal my aches
drowning in bottles
to calm my shakes
as the sun burns my temple
like holy water to a vampire

We see our always-slurring neighbor
downing a bottle of peppermint schnapps
at 10:50 am
wincing at the harsh sun streaming down on him
staggering, telling us he's en route to a job interview
at Chipotle.

Weed trimmer

A nameless garage in an industrial zone
by a Chinese restaurant donned Jackie Chan II,
juicy roach Christmas lights
koi tank in the window
the only hydration
in a desert of garage doors and warehouses

Inside one
perched cameras in corners,
bright lights and hydroponic gardens
bubbling brooks run down cement

i sit at a table with 12 white men
black light posters of aliens and pot leaves and mushrooms
that jumped off the wall and assumed human form
they talk THC wax and edibles and Snoop Dogg.
exuding shaggy hair, Phish shirt, Scooby Doo tee,
walking marijuana leaf logos inside fungus

i gift my rubber gloves to them after the picking
they store the finger hash like squirrels
in their blacklight cheeks
at lunch, boys run down to the creek
to poke themselves with fumes

i nibble a cookie and my elbow radiates
i have to go home and lay on the couch in dimness
until the sun stops moving throughout my body
constant skunk stink and jovial lyrics
from the breathing shrooms

All 20s,
but one 60

tie-dye shirted ,
reggae-obsessed white frog

We really bring a crowd to our show, he says
people love when we do instrumentals too, he says
last summer we played a shrimp festival, he says
the video is up on YouTube, he says
we had a music video on MTV, he says
yeah, we were really popular back then, he says
we got all kinds of girls back then, he says
hot ones too, he says
we went on tour and even got to go to Jamaica, he says
i was the only white guy
hanging out with the Rastafarians, he says
everyone was impressed
by how hard i ripped on the bong there, he says
slow down, they told me, he says
he chuckles, he burps, the blacklight boys are impressed
pretty fucked up what happened in France yesterday, i say
my band loves to talk about social issues, he says
we usually talk about
whatever social issue is the most popular, he says
before we play our last song, he says
it really gets the crowd going, he says
we are really looking for more gigs around here, he says
we really need some press

The manager tells him i am a music journalist
i regret showing the cleavage
of both my bulbous timelines
i just write a few stories a month for a paper, i say
it's nothing
i'm nothing

ignore me as you were
i want to melt into the flowers and get picked apart
crumbled into keef

He's the camera and he's recording this
you should write an article about my band, he says
how about this for an angle? he asks
this is a good one, he says
we have been around since the eighties, he says
we have done some big things, he says
we were on MTV, he says
that's really big, he says
it could really help your career, he says

i have interviewed Johnny Rotten and the Backstreet Boys and yet
i just left a job at Walmart
is why i want to say
what makes you think that you can help me?
what makes you think i care?
but i just smile and look down.

Sushi server

5 days a week,
12 hour shifts
but
i need the money
the upper in my working blood
was short-lived
like a cocaine high
stolen with back daggers

i am proud to say, that this lady
yes, me
has never stabbed anyone for blood
money, not even a penny,
no substance can submerge me in that ocean
but i do write about stabbings

i walk in for the interview
and see Him smiling sweetly on the phone
i wait like a puppy with big eyes,
he hangs up, i say my name and He frowns
"you work now,"
pointing with cut fingernails minus one long wizard dagger
he puts me on my leash

On mornings I clean up empty beer bottles
and glasses, sometimes broken
sweep cigarette butts off the floor
from His late-night poker parties
the times He turns magic tricks

By the end of the day
my legs begin to wilt
mind dulls to a butterknife

just yearning for bed, my holder
i look out the window
to see laser streams floating in the dark
i cannot wait to walk 8 blocks
alone in the dark
keys sticking through my fingers like claws
until the train
until i can be on lasers in the dark
until my stop, i walk two midnight blocks
put my key in the lock
and turn
walk upstairs like a stalling deer
so i can collapse on leather
legs, arms, and brain-flip jello
laugh lasers in the dark
then stand in the water
until the drops puncture, massage the hours
of rushing
of being yelled at

His wife is nicer,
on Fridays she comes and makes me soup
once she wore a tank top
i saw a gunshot scar on her shoulder

Days before
i was with a man shot in a movie theater
just miles away
asking him about the movie
well, not the actual movie
but that one it grew into

He yells at me so much

that sometimes customers slip me
extra money
a 20 here, a 5 here
before the bill, pre-tip
most people, people like me, only last a day
i train a boy with spider lashes and hazel gems
who spins webs in my sternum
he gets yelled out
for not memorizing the Santa Fe roll
so he rolls out the door with his finger in the air
then the phone rings
and he asks for my number
like him, like her, like they, they only last hours
not me
i'm programmed to fear being unemployed
because then i'll become invisible
and i'm not a quitter
i'm used to abuse and desperation, i protest
plus i sneak sips of free Sake from the machine
and i get free sushi, soy sauce, and rice
so i get something out of it
while it rips the bark off my body

One day though, it burns too much
and i am hungry and a little drunk
i throw my apron to the floor
and walk out into sunshine,
spite and freedom feel so good

What crappy job will I have next?
bring it on, i squint.

Bowling alley waitress

5 days a week,
12 hour shifts
but
i need the money

There's no thru line there
a train and a bus
or a pocket-hemorrhaging Lyft
i'll just cut it out of my paycheck
it's better than nothing
even if it's close to the povertyzone
i work in a funzone
in the bowling area
with painful lights
and shrill children screaming

Lane to lane
table to table
a sewer saucer on my flat hand
i'm a balancing queen
greasy fingers
just kissed by chicken wings, honey
garlic thumbs crammed into bowling ball holes
giant marbles of bacteria

Rugs dressed
like a 1980s nightmare
of triangles and squares and neon squiggles
of the tips of toes of teens
who don't tip
when the fluorescent lights go down
like the sun
and the disco flares

the music grinds
to my teeth

Neither are the parents
gratuitous, albeit extra
sometimes and often
a woman complains
to the manager about me
because i don't bring her a fork
she ordered a sandwich

The birthday parties
bring the most bread
mobs of parents and kids shouting orders
sodas and cheeseburgers
carbs, carbs, carbs, me and my children want carbs
and hot dogs and chili cheese fries
and Bud Lights—enter my brain like squiggles
i draw on my pad

My neon green shirt
reeks of french fries
chili cheese fries
i am here to take your order
in this windowless fun zone
full of hisses and beeps and plastic trees

Only one
knows i work here
only one
who i let in on my Walmart secret
knows i am employed inside
a bowling alley in Columbine

the same one
who people said i would go Columbine over
but became the one i went Sunflower for

My boss tells me I don't have to hide my gun
etched on my skin
in thick bleeding chunks
a tattoo i earned in the south
a literary "write to kill"
it helps my liberal ass pass as right wing if it suits me
but here everyone knows

i will not stick out so much here

All the camo in the alleys
hunting gear drip, and so much dip
swirling in empty soda cups tossed on the floor by the balls
mimicking murky coca-cola and thick

He tells us
warns us
that the place is haunted
by a variety of things
as abstract as the shapes on the rug
a dead girl in the go-cart area
a child who broke her neck
is stuck in the purgatoryzone
of the time it was a roller rink
a demonic spirit in the laser tag room, unexplained

Do not whistle when you come in that way
not in the morning, He warns
they will whistle back, He says

they may turn on the water faucets, don't be alarmed
three lanes are shut down permanently
also for haunting reasons, He says

It happened to me, only once
on New Year's Eve
the night i was tipped the most, $300
yelling songs with paralyzed feet
as tired as a mother organizing a bowling birthday

The mega boss, Mr. Clean in bouncer form
whose avatar form drips down our checks
dodges rumors
that the place will be bulldozed and rebuilt as a dental office
like Neo in the matrix
ducking under bullet, spiraling over another
only He doesn't look cool at all
we just need to know so we can prepare, one waitress says
i have a child to feed, she says
i want reassurance, she says
i can reassure you, He says
there are no plans for this place to shut down, He says
but the paper, she protests
don't believe everything you read, He maintains

The bowling alley has now been bulldozed
the dental office has risen from its haunted ashes
teeth are cleaned and whitened amid demonic spirits
magazines and books are read
as teeth await drilling and pulling
above the cursed lanes.

Newspaper reporter

Driving down deserted roads
trying to find a train derailment
an ambulance
a public radio reporter whirls a dramatic donut
and i follow them all
literally chasing an ambulance
eyes fastened to the red lights
shaking my head, laughing maniacally
toward a hill to climb
to talk to survivors
so, how was that train derailment?

One day i write a story about a man caught selling fentanyl
the next, he leaves a voicemail for the editor
i am going to walk in there, shoot you in the head
and then myself in the head, he says
this is not a crime, the police say
if a shooter comes in, everyone go to the back
that's the plan
what about the receptionist
is he just a lamb?

Gunfire erupts
the next day
just blocks away
by the pizza place
a social worker struck dead in daylight
to an audience eating pizza
before that, unknowingly
three women slaughtered in a farmhouse
they will become invisible
though all killed with the same shattered hand
as the one with a line around her head in thick marker

Become i, a liaison
an old bully becomes a source
to the shooting
to the name
i got the name
over the veterans
and every day forward
whenever there's a crime
i'm asked, what's the name?
if i don't know
eyes will roll
heads do roll
if you try too much
when you're platform pink

The shooter's daughter
compliments my shoes
i want to write for a job, she says
will you help me?
her current job is snatching purses
from the elderly, allegedly
be careful, they say
your tires could get slashed
your purse ripped away or worse
yeah, i know

The newsroom laughs at my jokes
with their backs turned to me
some acknowledge my work, albeit softly
with their backs turned to me
until just one man says stop
just one, again
one penis is equal to 73.3 vaginas, i did the math

ten years after the television news job
and five dollars an hour more

My Facebook becomes a collection
of murder victims' relatives
of murderers' relatives
of possible murderers
of drug dealers
of people raised
flawed, the same as the rest
just more outlined

Mostly i sit
in a room alone with a computer
or in a room alone with computers
in board meetings, in schools, in city centers
budget cuts and weeds on train tracks
will sheep be used or chemicals?

We can't get rid of the redemption center, one man cries
downtown reeks of cigarettes, another whimpers
we need a parking garage, a woman proclaims
a man tells me the newspaper is too negative
i have some story ideas, he says
write a story about my friend; he is 7 feet tall, he suggests
write a story about how wonderful the flowers
in town smell

Picking low hanging berries
man yelling about bees, naked man runs down Main Street
carrying toaster
for the police logs

for the laugh logs

Riding along with the police
who chew dip
and tell me not to tell anybody
i can't anyway, i signed a contract
i can report nothing but observe it all
like an Argus
i enter apartments and trailers while they arrest
those whose lives have slid like skin off the tracks
the puddles in their hearts now in arrest
not one person asks who this strange woman is
hanging out with police,
unarmed, wearing jeans and a fur hat
they look at me; i know they wonder
but they have bigger problems

Sitting in the courtroom
watching kids from my dingy playpen
plea for mercy, get punished, sometimes get mercy
all the dirt from the pen
soaking into my pen
one woman, one day, two heroin arrests

He tells me that i'm the only female reporter

He's ever known
that He hasn't seen cry
i never cry over a story, a subject, i say
when i did cry later
over my own body
He laughed

but i didn't shed a tear
when my newsroom career
was ripped to shreds
because i wrote about my body
on command, but not in the proper way—
fuck ⅓ of the newsroom, won't help
in this case

The mascot of this paper is too boring, i criticize
i think we should revise
it to a monster with hundreds of eyes
looking over town beyond the outskirts, watching
it will be very metal, i argue
we need something like this
for small town journalism to survive
i only half joke
i'm too much for them
i knew from the beginning
that they wanted me to be a boring logo or disappear
and like many terms of employment
when i get too pink
just on the brink of crimson red
i vanish into thin air

The perfume i left behind
has been vacuumed out
like i was never there
but you can locate my prints,
and whiffs
if you look and smell around, news kittens.

**Barista/bartender
at a college cafe/bar**

Getting up when the sky is still pink
again
makes me think
i am not mediocre
again
makes me feel as rare as the Northern Lights
on a southern cloudy evening
while the sun's still purging

Giant panes of glass
let in the sun
as it rises
eggs dance inside silicone rings
bacon swims in the air
melding with coffee
as i froth
as i think
and wait for the clock to strike
and let in all the students
like me

The children's lit majors prefer tea
morning and night
sometimes wine

The adult lit writers chug coffee
morning and night
lots of whisky, wine, vodka, beer, anything

MFA in music students
...same

Carrying buckets of ice through art exhibits
statues of birds
when the sun is yellow
i like being on the upside down of the school
the worker to the students
the snow bee to the driveway

i am too
when in classroom the register is overturned
i can smell the dead pigs seeping through the vents
suffocating me with their gas, their ghastly gasping
the see-saw helps me write.

Sidenote

// i've been working since 6 am
and my boyfriend is sleeping
at 11
he's sleeping
his phone keeps ringing
it's his job
honey, it's X calling
i'm his receptionist every morning
the days his phone is on
he answers, says, yes I'm doing x and x
i'm working from home but just finishing up, goodbye
he rolls over and goes back to sleep
3 hours later he's home again, playing Everquest
he is promoted
i am degraded

// i am sleeping with my coworker
he loves my work
wow they really criticize your work more than mine
or any other guy, he points out
i would not point this out
because i know i'll get pointed *at*
later, i break up with him
for unrelated reasons
one boy, 4229 cups

i try to stay his friend
or even fuckfriend
but he says it's either girlfriend
or dead to him
and that's how he became
THEY too
now he also hates my work

// Obviously, he can send emails
without exclamation points
i cannot
!!!
he can end conversations without
thank you so much!!
or fix situations without
ooh, i'm sorry, my bad!
i get reprimanded for a bad attitude
if i try to exude
a professional attitude
a confident altitude
like the men told me to

Act like a boss
if you're male
you'll be treated like a boss

Act like a boss
if you're not
you'll be treated like a woman

Remember exclamation points
lessen the ballsy blow, boss
when trying to get your point across

// A boss in the boardroom
but a baby in the bedroom
&
a baby in the kitchen
&
a baby in the living room
&

a baby when there are boobs around

I am weak, He says
yet I need to be the boss
I need to
I just have to
but for you I am just
          helpless

Dote on them
at home
like their mommy does
who they don't even call on Mother's Day
don't forget to call your mom, the receptionist says
babies forever
who can't cook an egg
or tie their own shoelaces
but can destroy the lives of 10 people
if they so wish
bosses like that flood the boardroom
the control room
the newsroom
all sorts of rooms.

Crime writer

Finally, i can Google
and Google hard
serial killers, mass shooters, cannibals, corpses
moms who kill their sons, sons who kill their moms,
people who stab the one they
(claim to) love in the back
people who shoot
their spouse in the head
i get paid for it,
and have an excuse
in case anyone checks my searches
being sick is my job now, thank you very much
researching the most disgusting animal of all
is my life's work
though sometimes i wish i could submerge
instead of skim

My (retired) boyfriend
who owns 15 guns
half of which are machine guns
tells me to stop
please for the love of nature, full stop
stop watching those shows
about murder and death
and listening to those podcasts
with men giggling about blood gurgling
please, when you're not at work
stop looking at the grotesque

No
no, it doesn't affect me
no, it doesn't disturb me
look outside, don't you see the spiders weaving webs

and cats fighting over a dead rat
when they have Fancy Feast at home
and hands to pet them
hearts that love them
stop acting like this planet doesn't have zits
and you'll be less disturbed by
all of it.

Writer

It used to be a challenge
to boil down all the sauce
into one serving
covering all the solids
there's so, so much of it all

Now i am used to putting parts
of me down the drain
lots of me down the tube
shoving organs down
letting the garbage disposal rip them apart
me to bits
shred my soul, devour my arteries
i don't need it all out there
but i need a lot of it out there
trust me,
i have a lot of guts to give

i'm radiating so hard
all the gills in my body are venting
so i don't explode
it always feels like i'm going to, regardless

i let out as much steam as i can
without a blast
and form it into words
while the core keeps formulating more,
alone in a cave
flickering memories prevent me from accelerating
sucking them from my skin
transferring them onto my screen

I am breathing

this is my breathing machine
I need it to survive
I need it, or only my body lives.

Dedicated to all the shitty ass bosses I had, in particular:
-One who shamed me for writing an article about rape
-One who ignored my complaints of sexual harassment
-Slimer, boss of my heart, who has been ghosting me recently

More genuinely, dedicated to everyone out there in the workplace. You are valuable, even if you aren't valued. Thank you to all the cool bosses I've ever had as well as the following people for their support in various ways which have not gone unnoticed by me:

Chrystin Ondersma for always supporting and encouraging me as a friend and as a writer (I'm not worthy!), my step mom Ann Mahony Cook, my brother Matthew Conn (even though he assures me he hasn't really been that supportive), Ryan Cayia, my wonderful cousins Nicole, Jessica and Michelle Spinelli and Bernadette Trefilio as well as my eggstra supportive cousin Margaret Conn, Nathalie Kraynina, Ruta Miniotas, Lynn Ayer, one of my favorite bosses ever Gina Pace, Tobias Micah Krause, Hannah Palmer Egan, Rachel Feldman, Mikki Shea, Becky Gollin, Ric Nudell, Peter Tiso, Mario Fontana, Matt Cook, Adam Lash, Royal Young, William Seward Bonnie (rest in Space Jam), Suzi Boeglin, Ben Karge, Arielle Roberts, Nick Mamatas, Alexandra Kostoulas, Tameca Coleman, Hillary Leftwich, Jay Halsey, Madi Chamberlain, Dustin Holland, Erica Back, Frank Smecker, Jennifer Jarecki, Annette Bisson Rossi and family, Debra Gould, Abigayle Smith, Missy Wiggins, Anna Brooks, Bianca Viñas, Lindsay Gacad; former rad boss Jana Markow, Garrett Heaney, Caleb Teske and Tasha Baker, Maggie Lenz, Jeffrey Levine at Tupelo Press, VCFA staff and former professors especially Miciah Bay Gault, Julianna Baggott and fellow alumnx: Brianna Stallings, Dan Cretano, Jennifer Kathleen Gibbons, Jad Yassine, Breanne Cunningham, Tierney Ray, Jeremy Wolf as well as good pals Mary Lynn Ritch, Erin Riley, Kim Vodicka, Bryanna Doe Singer, Barracuda Guarisco, Josh Dudley, Joshua Robert Long, Sarah Madison, Maggie Craig and Papercut Press and all the talented pressmates at Vegetarian Alcoholic Press as well as Tarpaulin Sky Press homies M. Forajter and Christian Peet. There are countless others who have supported me and my writing that I have not included, partially because I don't have enough room on this page but mainly because my brain is as saturated as a gin-soaked shrimp. Please forgive me and continue to employ me as your friend and deranged writer.

Most importantly, I want to thank my wonderful freditor, Freddy La Force, for his love and support and for believing in me enough to publish my poetry: a dream since I was a shrimpling. Also I would like to thank the Shrimpstreet Boyz for sending me a lifetime supply of fried shrimp.

Gina Tron has authored several books, including *You're Fine.* (2014), *Eggolio and Other Fables* (2015), and *Star 67* (2020). Her forthcoming memoir, *Suspect*, won the 2020 Tarpaulin Sky Press book award. Her words have been published in *Green Mountains Review, Hunger Mountain, Junto Magazine* and *Tupelo Press*. Gina has an MFA in Writing and Publishing from the Vermont College of Fine Arts. In addition to writing true crime content for *Oxygen*, her reporting has been in the *Washington Post, VICE, Daily Beast* and *Politico*.

Blooper Reel

Dorm drug dealer

Frayed pants
wet at the bottom
living in a castle of bottles
and mold
a drawer full of mushrooms
my fridge is an empty room
my walls are bleeding the finality
of the previous stage
zombies drawn to the room
like ants to sugar water
overdosing on PCP
I'm a car driving through snowy streets
actually it's ash
there's been an explosion
from deep in my cerebral
I'm no Tony Montana
I'm more like Pookie
but still,
I attract wannabees
I fuck two men who
claim to have killed
one of them, maybe
he had a ring to prove it
now he's vanished from this earth
never to have existed
blank like my fridge
blank like my notebooks
and lined paper
only folded around drugs
until an April dip
a May trip, empty room
into Clonazepam closet
and then ants in all crevices

no top sheet
comforter over my brain
blankets only exist
over the volcanos
between my eyes, my toes, my memories
and now I can't
even drink a can of Coke
without a gasp for air
a putter in the heart
ancient butterflies attempting to fly up
malnourished and misinformed
get caught in tar, die in my throat
faded pink flowers in the vase
turn a vibrant shade of coral
like a flip of a light, spikes all through my veins
roses spinning out of control
kickstarting the wilt.

Weekend

I sit on the rug in my bedroom
the Sunday sun cascading in onto my faux zebra fur rug
I am melting into it
enjoying the rays of the television
zapping the shell of my heart

Get up, my mom tells me, each weekend
you can't be lazy
you have to be productive

You can't be lazy
you have to be productive
I parent myself now
decades later
on a holy morning still
as my body and heart
crave to sink
ache to relax.

CPSIA information can be obtained
at www.ICGtesting.com
Printed in the USA
LVHW081704040122
707835LV00015B/2387